REFLECTIONS FOR RADIANT LIVING

Prayers for the Heart

✳✳✳

BY HEATHER HAVEY, M.A.

Transcendence Press
Sebastian, FL

www.peacethroughkindness.com

Copyright © 2008, Heather Havey, M.A.

All rights reserved. Printed in the United States of America. No portion of this publication may be reproduced in any manner without written permission of the publisher.

Cover designed by Heather Havey;
Cover photograph by Devon Mickey

To see more of Devon Mickey's art and green building, please visit **www.ourbelovedearth.com**

ISBN 978-0-6152-2272-1
Printed in the United States of America

Transcendence Press
Sebastian, FL 32958

Please visit our website at
www.peacethroughkindness.com

FIRST EDITION 2008

Aloha.

**May these prayers touch your heart
as they touch mine,
and may they add warmth and peace
to your day, for you are sacred.**

When you read each prayer or sacred quote or poem, please take your time. Be unoccupied, and allow space, for that is where you can behold God, within yourself and all life. Let the prayers sink in. Speak each one like a mantra or visualization for your life. Sing it if you'd like. Share it with a friend. Feel your own unique experiences. Agree or disagree. This book honors all paths and experiences. You can read one page a day, one page a week, the whole thing in one sitting, a sentence here and there while you are taking a bath, keep it in your purse for moments when you are stuck in traffic, or anytime you would like to pick it up.

There is nothing new in this book, but it is filled with the teachings of saints and bodhisattvas that shine forth as spiritual truths in all periods of history. I hope you enjoy it.

I am grateful beyond words for my guru Ma Jaya Sati Bhagavati, paramaguru Neem Karoli Baba, and vital spiritual teachers: Jesus, Mother Teresa, Jaya Devi Bhagavati, Coretta Scott King, Martin Luther King Jr., Gandhi, Thich Nhat Hanh, Buddha, and many others.

Thank you, also, to my sweet Belle, Papa, Chris, Pancake, Jomo, Monkey, Angel, Joan, Charli and Tasha, Amy, GB, Sefick, and all my friends whom I love dearly.

"God is in the sharing." –Neem Karoli Baba

A little word in kindness spoken,
A motion or a tear,
Has often healed the heart that's broken,
And made a friend sincere.
– William Wordsworth

*   *   *

The experience of the presence of God is available and within at all times, but awaits choice. That choice is made only by surrendering everything other than peace and love to God. In return, the divinity of the Self reveals Itself as ever present but not experienced only because it has been ignored or forgotten, or because one has chosen otherwise.
– David R. Hawkins, *The Eye of the I*

Warmth Expands, Coldness Contracts

Friends, we always have the freedom of choice.

May we choose words and actions that honor self and others. Such choices make others feel warm and valuable, rather than hurt or flawed or dispensable. This is a path of consciously choosing respect, kindness, and non-judgment. It is a path of conscious non-harm.

Warmth expands; coldness contracts. Warmth adds and grows, while coldness shrinks and inhibits. Both are parts of the world. This is the nature of the world of forms.

In each moment we bear a gift - the power to spread warmth or coldness. The most simple and perfect example is a smile for someone you see. Do this without expecting or needing a particular response in return from them; do it simply to give, not to receive. We do not need to butter people up with compliments and positive evaluations; we need simply be present and value them. This will naturally lead us to warm but not saccharine or fake responses. Everyone has a wounded heart. We can give or receive anything. Loving-kindness is the most healing, biggest, and highest power that anyone can give or receive.

We add joy to this world through our example and choices. May we expand and expand, until we realize that we are the trees, we are the leaves, we are male and female, we are the music, we are the stars, we are part of all that exists, we are God.

Late have I loved thee, O Beauty so ancient and so new; late have I loved thee! For behold, thou wert within me and I outside; and I sought thee outside and in my unloveliness fell upon these lovely things that thou hast made. Thou wert with me and I was not with thee. I was kept from thee by those things, yet had they not been in thee, they would not have been at all. Thou didst call and cry to me and break open my deafness. . . . I tasted thee, and now hunger and thirst for thee; thou didst touch me, and now I burn for thy peace.
– Saint Augustine

* * *

The breath of the flute player...
Does it belong to the flute?
– Rumi, II 1793

A Place Called Home

God created you from love, and this is your deepest essence. You contain every potential within, from smallest to largest, though you tend to view yourself as small. May God bless you with a vision that you are far more than you have imagined: you are Divine. Truly you are everything. There is no separation. It is not possible. Knowing this brings great peace to your heart.

May you feel God's warm and tender touch upon your heart, so that you may also walk through life with a gentle step and humble regard.

God, may we please experience your arms of love, and may we know that this is a place we can call home, for it is your creation, and we are all your creation, your play, your Self.

God is your true refuge, your home. You cannot believe this, beyond hopefulness, until you experience it directly, but once you do, you will never forget. There are ways to see, beginning with: when you bite an apple, feel how it blesses and heals you. When you breathe, or feel the sun on your skin, feel what a gift it is and let it heal you. Realization of God's presence heals you more than anything else, and it also changes your life. Everything that once seemed mundane or profane, you now see as sacred and worth so much gratitude and care. It is given to you freely, without demand that you notice or care. Once you experience all of this, then you can begin to trust, let go, and relax more deeply.

I am a little pencil in the hand of a writing God who is sending a love letter to the world.
– Blessed Mother Teresa of Calcutta

* * *

Every time you smile at someone, it is an action of love, a gift to that person, a beautiful thing.
– Blessed Mother Teresa of Calcutta

* * *

Love is the beauty of the soul.
– Saint Augustine

Live Aloha

Friends, may we create and envision a world filled with the Hawaiian spirit of aloha...This includes:

Akahai - Kindness, expressed with tenderness.
Lokahi - Unity, expressed with harmony.
Olu'olu - Agreeableness, expressed with pleasantness.
Ha'aha'a - Humility, expressed with modesty.
Ahonui - Patience, expressed with perseverance.

The Hawaiian people, like other Native peoples, believe in living with simplicity, close to nature, with kindness toward all forms of life - respecting all life as Divine. For these and many other native peoples, there is no differentiation between sacred and profane.

For most westerners, it is a practice and a great challenge even to imagine that life is alive and sacred. Most of us have never even had that experience, which is a tragedy, as it is a view into the depth of our connectedness and Divinity. Most westerners unfortunately view life as separate, lonely, and lifeless resource meant only for human consumption and profit. No wonder so many people are lonely and depressed.

As we look around at the world and plants and people around us, let us practice - then - approaching everything with friendliness, gratitude, and care – may we see our deep connectedness...for these indeed are the heart of aloha.

The grapes of my body can become wine
after the winemaker tramples me.
I surrender my spirit like grapes to his trampling
so my inmost heart can blaze and dance with joy.
– Rumi

Embrace Life

May we learn to receive and enjoy life, as the orchard receives the rain, which then grows in thanksgiving.

May we learn to embrace life, as the waters that fall and kiss the earth, which then allow horses to drink, plants to unfold in leafy celebration, children to play in mud puddles in the South Carolina sun....

> The more we embrace, the more joy we feel.
> The more joy we feel, the more we embrace.

The spirit down here in man and
the spirit up there in the sun,
in reality are only one spirit,
and there is no other one.
– *The Upanishads*

*   *   *

Seeing, hearing and feeling are miracles,
and each part and tag of me is a miracle.
– Walt Whitman

*   *   *

There are only two ways to live your life.
One is as though nothing is a miracle.
The other is as if everything is.
– Albert Einstein

Miracles

May we allow the miraculous to enter and fill the everyday.

When we see that life is a continuous unfolding of miracles, then we can embrace such gifts as possibility, imagination, letting go, and a playful spirit. Then we do not need to be so serious about everything, even though we may care even more than ever before.

From this awareness, may we be able to experience deep care in each moment, regardless of circumstance. The natural result of such an orientation is the ongoing thought, "How may I serve the life before me?" rather than always "Me first. What about me? What can I get from this person? How can I dominate them or be better than them?"

"What about me" is the cry of pain that someone feels when they have not fully realized their divinity (most of us)...but "we" is the song of the one who has glimpsed the vast divinity of life. Peace fills the heart, and joy fills the body when beholding the diverse play of sacred forms. Then we can be free of evaluation and push-pull, more alive, present, centered in stillness and peace, and we turn to God for all proofs and needs.

One natural result of seeing miracles is deep devotion to the well-being of all life. Look closely, and ask God to be able to see. Each breath, the texture of a blade of grass, sunlight on your face, beholding a squirrel holding and chewing a nut - each part of life is an infinite miracle.

Life consists in what a man is thinking of all day.
– Ralph Waldo Emerson

* * *

What the caterpillar calls the end,
the rest of the world calls a butterfly.
– Lao Tzu

Blessing Thoughts

May we allow our gaze to be spacious like the sky - a clear, wide-open view - that observes thoughts like passing clouds, without latching on to them with terror or demands or reactions - simply observing, with our hearts focused always on God. To do this, allow space in your day. Don't fill it up so much with chaotic thoughts or millions of things to do.

For this whole day, this whole week, your whole life, closely notice - What do you pay most attention to?

Is it how blessed you are to be able to walk down a street and watch leaves and limbs move against a cloudy sky? How blessed you are to breathe in clean air? Do you notice birds, or how the plants grow? Do you hear how the insects sing? Do you notice the moon? Do you notice the people around you? Do you tend to think - "Are they happy? Do they need something?" - or do you think - "Look at all these morons. - or - What can they do for me? Nothing? Then I don't have time for their nonsense." Do you notice mostly how hard life is, or how bad your own luck has been? Do you feel alone in a sea of mean or ignorant or dramatic people?

All thoughts are a wake-up call. Walk toward the light. What I mean is, if you have a repeating negative thought, then observe what it is expressing to you: a need for some small or large change. Often the change needed is a change of internal belief. Sometimes chronic negative thoughts are a personal addiction designed to feel powerful as a victim or martyr...but please know that you are not a victim and this is merely a limiting role that you have chosen, often to try to manipulate others into taking care of you or to try to feel special in some way. You do not need to prove your specialness to yourself or to others. If we need help from someone, we can directly ask them. They may not know how to read our signs or our unspoken ways of calling out for help. No matter what you have done or what you have gone through, no matter what anyone says or thinks, God created you and sustains you, and you are sacred. You do not need to wear the cloak of victim or martyr or insignificance any longer.

Our experiences, no matter how challenging or unfair they may have been or may still be, can give us deep compassion for others who are going through similar or worse things. Then we can use our passionate energy for service and care, rather than on whining and a very small and painful view of life. You are a survivor in life, not a victim.

So, may we choose thoughts that bless and honor, rather than thoughts of judgment and smallness.

Bless Life Rather Than Curse Life

May we bless the world rather than curse the world.

Love is what everyone wants and needs most.

May we learn to touch life, and when we notice things that seem awry or difficult, and even when we notice the miracles, may we send blessings to all these aspects of life, through either thinking, "God bless you, sweet dying tree" –

or - walk through a store and for every person you pass, even ones who cut you off or scowl @ you, think of a prayer or blessing and express it inwardly, as an intention for their well-being (for actively suffering people need blessings even more) –

or - through our actions - "Yes, I shall notice this woman who can barely carry her groceries, and I shall carry them for her"...or "Yes, I care about those whom most people overlook, and I would be honored to go visit with people who are dying and alone, or volunteer in a homeless shelter each week, or simply pick up trash in someone's yard" or "Yes, I shall devote my life to environmental conservation, because I see the species dying and I care about them" or "Yes, I shall leave anonymous gifts for friends sometimes simply because they'd enjoy it."

I wish I could show you,
When you are lonely or in darkness,
The Astonishing Light
of your own Being.
– Hafiz

The Light of your Own Beauty

Sometimes we feel afraid, or doubtful, or angry, or frustrated. There is a season for everything, and all feelings are natural.

May we choose to believe in tenderhearted care for self and all life. No one deserves pain, but we all experience it to varying degrees and in diverse ways. We can use our pain and our passion as fuel to create something beautiful - even - and especially - when we've been harmed. This is a lesson that I have learned from my most important spiritual teachers, notably the great guru Ma Jaya Sati Bhagavati: use it as fuel.

All challenges are opportunities to expand one's perception and to gain more compassion.

As they say in the movie Cousins: "We can either make our life chicken shit or chicken salad: which will you choose"?

When you sit before me,
even if you are a drooling mess,
My eyes sing with Excitement --
They see your Divine Worth.
— Hafiz

*   *   *

We do not believe in ourselves until someone reveals that deep inside us is something valuable, worth listening to, worthy of our trust, sacred to our touch. Once we believe in ourselves we can risk curiosity, wonder, spontaneous delight or any experience that reveals the human spirit.
— E. E. Cummings

You Are Divine

May our judgments become compassion.

Our viewpoint and our choices are often based upon very limited information, and as a result we often make mistakes or create harm, even when we do not intend to.

The biggest limitation we face is that many of us have not ever been shown the depths of our own beauty. Anger, jealousy, fear, sadness, and so much pain arise from not having deeply glimpsed the infinite depths of our own beauty - and our infinite connection, oneness, with all that exists. As the beloved Ma Jaya Sati Bhagavati says, "Jealousy is the lack of seeing your own beauty." This applies to many negative reactions we may have in our lives.

So let us be quick to say "I'm sorry," and "Will you please help me to understand?" or "How may I serve you?" for our view is so obscured by small-mindedness and negativity. The mind faithfully tries to help us, but the universe is SO much bigger than the brain, so let us watch the thoughts like clouds, but remember that we are the world - more than can ever be imagined in our wildest dreams.

May you rest in a deep peace and enjoyment this day knowing that you are one with All That Is.

I found in me all things forgotten, my own self forgotten, and awareness of thee, God, alone…I found myself in nature just like thee; I found myself in nature one with thee…O Eternal Light of Divine Glory, since thou are in my innermost depths, since thou transcendest all things, be to me that thou art, a turning away from all things, into the ineffable Good that thou art in my naked self.
– Meister Eckhart

*   *   *

There was a Chinese farmer. One of his horses escaped from the pen and ran away; his neighbor said, "How awful." The farmer answered, "Maybe." The next morning, the horse returned with several other horses; his neighbor said, "How wonderful!" The farmer answered, "Maybe." The farmer's son tried to tame the wild horses, got thrown off and broke his leg; his neighbor said, "How terrible!" The farmer said, "Maybe." The next day the Chinese army came through trying to draft people into the military, and they did not choose the farmer's son because his leg was broken; his neighbor said, "How wonderful!" The farmer said, "Maybe."
– Author Unknown, "The Maybe Parable"

We Are Held In Arms Of Love

We are held in arms of love. Every bite, every fragrant and moonlit night, every friend, every wrestling match, every breath, every intact organ, is a gift.

May we try to remember – that everything around us – is a miracle and a gift. On a day when our mind or experience is occupied with drama or difficulty or chaos, it may be more difficult to see. On other days, when our mind and eyes are more clear and present, then when we look around our hearts overflow with gratitude and wonder.

May we also share these – the joy, the thankfulness, and the awareness – with those around us. This is the greatest gift we can give – to share love and joy, to notice others and what they may need in a moment.

When we feel that we need love, then give love to yourself or to someone else. This will fill your moment with love, and it will come from the Divine source within your own heart – not from an external source as we are used to expecting or wanting.

A morning bath by my River soothes the day
That is yet to begin
The naked flesh begins free of sin
The River waters – always to dry in the sun
A clean, simple cloth spread upon the body
And the puja's done…
My River, you are the light of my heart
– Beloved Ma Jaya Sati Bhagavati, from *The River*

*   *   *

And I, infinitesimal being,
Drunk with the great starry void,
Likeness, image of mystery,
I felt myself a pure part of the abyss,
I wheeled with the stars,
My heart broke free on the open sky.
– Pablo Neruda

You Are The River

Ma Jaya Sati Bhagavati teaches of the sacred River. It is reflected in the river Ganges of India, in which people bathe and pray everyday of their lives. To Hindu people the river can cleanse a person's soul of all their karmas and past mistakes. The River flows from the Heavens and can purify the hearts of all the people. It represents the love of God flowing through your own heart, when you open yourself up to that reality as a possibility. When you open your heart to possibility, then it may become actuality. Your whole life can change.

God's love flows around and through us like a river every second. May you step into the River, that Its pure love may flow through and from your heart.

When we open our heart and mind fully in the moment, when we are unoccupied with thoughts, then we can become a receptacle for God's love to pass through us into the world.

All people hold this ability and this gift within their hearts. We need to become aware of these deeper, richer levels of life.

May we taste the rich nectar of being alive.

Who has not found the heaven below
Will fail of it above.
God's residence is next to mine,
His furniture is love.
– Emily Dickinson

*   *   *

Life is love and love is life...What is desire, but love of the self? What is fear but the urge to protect? and what is knowledge but the love of truth? The means and forms may be wrong, but the motive behind is always love - love of the me and the mine. The me and the mine may be small, or may explode and embrace the universe, but love remains.
– Sri Nisargadatta Maharaj, *I Am That*

Love Is All There Is

There is nothing that you have to do or be or hold onto. Simply know that all life is sacred. Then you can begin to know your own beauty and know your own sacredness.

May we surrender every idea of what we are and what we should be and rest in that wide creative field of Beingness. When we exist this way, we feel a wide sky deep within our hearts. It feels like intense joy, like being very high up in the clouds, observing but not attached to forms of your life, flying through beauty and discovery. This energy flows into, through, and all around us. From this experience, we begin to know Freedom. We see that there is no separation.

Love is God;
God is everything;
love is all there is.
Even fear...is love of the self.
Love is all there is.

The Book: It's an important and popular fact that things are not always what they seem. For instance, on the planet Earth, Man had always assumed that he was the most intelligent species occupying the planet, instead of the *third* most intelligent. The second most intelligent were of course dolphins. Dolphins had long known of the impending destruction of earth and had on many occasions tried to alert mankind but their warnings were mistakenly interpreted as amusing attempts to punch footballs or whistle for tidbits.
– Douglas Adams, *The Hitchhiker's Guide to the Galaxy*

Silliness

May we allow more space for silliness this week, that we may enjoy ever more possibility, plurability, pancakability, and other sillabilicus potentialis. Lightheartedness is a natural effect of en-"light"-enment. Enlightenment is the filling up of your life with light. This makes your step lighter, your heart lighter, your approach toward life lighter, your responses to situations lighter, and generally makes for a more pleasant existence.

There is Heaven in a smile...

and our ability to enjoy life is a sacred art.

Standing quietly by the fence,
You smile your wondrous smile.
I am speechless, and my senses are filled
By the sounds of your beautiful song.
Beginningless and endless.
I bow deeply to you
– Thich Nhat Hanh,
speaking to a flower

*   *   *

By cultivating one's nature
one will return to virtue.
– Chuang Tzu

Honor All Life

May we humbly bow to each moment…and say, "O gracious one, will you please show me your Divinity? Will you please teach me to surrender to You – Source of all Life, O most pure and tender Love?"

May we honor and serve all life, with loving-kindness. This starts with honoring yourself and then learning to honor others – people, animals, plants, sky, air, earth, water, all life, each moment. This is our journey and our challenge. It begins with learning to love yourself and then the life immediately around you. From there, your identity can expand outward and simultaneously inward into your own heart. As you go within in spiritual contemplation, then you also discover and connect with the entire world around you.

If you beat yourself up for all your imperfections, please try to stop. As one of my most beautiful spiritual teachers, Jaya Devi Bhagavati, once said to her students, "Why would you give up on you when you need you the most?" If you beat others up for what you perceive as their imperfections, please try to stop. Simply try to give yourself that which you demand or seek from others, and the journey will begin from that step. It is all within, and realizing that will bring you everywhere.

The true saint goes in and out amongst the people and eats and sleeps with them and buys and sells in the market and marries and takes part in social intercourse, and never forgets God for a single moment.
– Abu Sa'id

Never Forget God

May we remember God with every breath.

May we breathe in deeply and say, "Yes" and "Thank you." May we breathe in deeply and say, "God... God... God" over and over, forever.

We can use our fingers to remember God. Use the thumb to touch each joint on your other four fingers (three joints per finger) and, for each touch, speak the name of your Beloved. You can do this for a minute a day, or thirty minutes, or all day everyday, forever.

May we never forget our source and sustenance and essence.

The capacity to give one's attention to a sufferer
is a very rare and difficult thing. It is almost a miracle.
It is a miracle.
– Simone Weil

      *   *   *

May all beings everywhere,
Plagued with sufferings of body and mind,
Obtain an ocean of happiness and joy
By virtue of the bodhisattva's merits.
– Shantideva, from the *Bodhicharyavatara*

      *   *   *

Charity sees the need,
not the cause.
– German proverb

Compassion

In stature may we be like mountains, in movement like great streams; may we be as humble and serviceable as a cow, as impartially beneficent as the sun…

And from this space, may we honor and serve the life before us - seeing the strength, ability, possibility, and divinity within all life and within oneself.

Have thy heart in heaven
and thy hands upon the earth.
Ascend in piety and descend in charity.
For this is the Nature of Light
and the way of the children of it.
– Thomas Vaughan

     *   *   *

I regard not the outside and the words,
I regard the inside and the state of the heart.
I look at the heart if it be humble,
Though the words may be the reverse of humble.
Because the heart is substance, and words accidents,
Accidents are only a means,
substance is the final cause.
How long will thou dwell on words and superficialities?
A burning heart is what I want; consort with burning!
Kindle in the heart the flame of love,
and burn up utterly thoughts and fine expressions.
– Rumi

Love is Compassionate Action

May we "kindle in the heart the flame of love."

May we burn with passion that becomes compassionate action. Passion is vital life energy. We can use our passionate energy to strengthen any possible aspect of our lives – from the most harmful to the most healing. When the heart (care) is coupled with one's intuitive wisdom, then our core energy and actions can be very powerful agents for healing.

Passion without conscious choice can be harmful or obsessive, and compassion without action can break our hearts with pain. However, passion directed by conscious choice, compassion put into caring action, is a great gift of love.

When you commit to the practice of silence, your relationship to the entire universe changes. Your communication deepens and extends. Your meaning is carried by the breath and by the wind. There is no more difference between inner and outer. Earth and heaven meet where your heart and mind meet in silent bliss.
– Paul Ferrini, *The Silence of the Heart*, p. 13

The Stillness Within

May we sit by a tree, or with our feet in a stream, or floating on your back on the ocean, with eyes on our Beloved, wherever the heart calls us – breathe in deeply and feel the vast silence of the sacred heart within. This is the "sky of the heart"– the infinite love that pours through us and all life.

This deep inner silence is the true source of all strength – all love – all wisdom – all that is. It is the sacred heart of Jesus, whose gaze is always on His Beloved, God. Our hearts are the same, once we become still enough and empty enough to behold our Beloved within our own heart and within all life.

If you notice, animals have much more silence than we do. Watch a dog or a cat. Animals observe and communicate much more than we do within that silent space.

Each day may we take moments to be still. This is meditation; this is deep listening, deep connection to life. It can improve the quality of your life, because it will improve your ability to be calm and present in a moment.

When we judge ourselves we break our own hearts.
— Ty Mahadev Bittner

*   *   *

Peter Parker: Whatever comes our way, whatever battle we have raging inside us, we always have a choice...It's the choices that make us who we are, and we can always choose to do what's right.
— *Spiderman 3*

*   *   *

Nothing in the world is the way it ought to be. It's harsh, and cruel. But that's why there's us. Champions. It doesn't matter where we come from, what we've done or suffered, or even if we make a difference. We live as though the world were as it should be, to show it what it can be.
— Angel, from the TV series, "Angel," speaking to his son Connor

Conscious Choice

The mind tries to help protect and serve us, but it is a three-pound mass of cells that has collected limited experiences and perspectives – how can we expect it to come to accurate conclusions?

Life is far vaster than the mind can conceive.

May we breathe in the sacred silence of this moment and observe life from the space of the soul. Then we can see that we always – every moment – have a choice: to choose from the level of mind or from the level of soul.

Learn to choose more often from the space of the soul. This choice will expand your life into deeper love and connection.

Let us not be justices of the peace,
but angels of peace.
– Saint Thérèse of Lisieux

*   *   *

Love all that has been created by God, both the whole and every grain of sand. Love every leaf and every ray of light. Love the beasts and the birds, love the plants, love every separate fragment. If you love each separate fragment, you will understand the mystery of the whole resting in God.
– Fyodor Dostoyevsky

*   *   *

It is great wisdom to know how to be silent
and to look at neither the remarks, nor the deeds,
nor the lives of others.
– Saint John of the Cross

Be An Angel Of Peace

May we cease to judge others' choices, lives, and responses and choose instead acceptance, compassion, and peace.

Judgment is one of our mind's ways of trying to protect us, but it actually creates feelings of division and superiority. Also, it hurts people's feelings and can deeply wound their hearts if their value comes from others' opinions.

Measuring, comparing, and evaluating can help us to build a new home, but when it comes to others' actions and feelings, may we try to approach with humility, because we may not see the whole picture, or understand the past that has shaped their choice-making, or know if something is a blessing or a curse, or know what God has in store for them. May we let go of our absolutism and "knowingness" for these tend to be "better than thou" positionalities that divide people and make everyone feel bad.

We do not serve anyone - self or other - by judging another being or by thinking that we know what is best for them. May we surrender all this, everything, in prayer to the Universe, and ask God for guidance in all that we do.

We do not need to be someone's taskmaster of justice.

Instead, may we be stewards of peace.

It is the mind that makes one wise or ignorant,
bound or emancipated.
– Sri Ramakrishna

    *   *   *

If a pickpocket meets a holy man,
he will see only his pockets.
– Baba Hari Dass

Vision

      May we know that we are far, far more than our thoughts tell us that we are. As we realize this, let us bow down to the God in all life, in awe and thanksgiving.

      Thoughts will always by nature limit our lives, especially negative ones. Replace mental thoughts with this one vital remembrance: God, God, God, God.

      If your God is nature: Earth, Ocean, Birds…

      If your God is Christ: Christ, Christ, Christ…

      If your God is love: Love, Love, Love…

      Pray this prayer, and remember…on and on, forever.

...we must first inspire ourselves by discovering our true passion in life, by being true to our deeper Self.
— David Frawley, *Hymns from the Golden Age*, 209

            *   *   *

Everything'll be just fine, everything'll be all right, Live right now – Just be yourself – It doesn't matter if it's good enough for someone else.
— Jimmy Eat World

            *   *   *

May all your trails be crooked, winding, lonesome, dangerous, leading to the most amazing view...where something strange and more beautiful and full of wonder than your deepest dreams waits for you.
— Edward Abbey

Follow Your Heart

May we live with courage and feel the strength of passion and love fill our hearts and bodies.

May we remember the courage of our heroes, whomever they may be – Christ, Buddha, Gandhi, Martin Luther King, Mother Teresa, the saints, Granny D, the dolphins who save people's lives, your mother, and so on. They are our heroes because they reflect values and dreams that reside within our own heart, also.

By following the Heart, we share our deepest aliveness and beauty with the world. Trust and follow your heart, because it is God's message to you for your life.

A state of mind free from all desires is love,
and love is God.
– Baba Hari Dass

*   *   *

Q: How should we show love to others?
A: If you have love inside, it will spread everywhere. Love can't be made and shown if there is no love in our hearts. If there is love inside us we don't need to show it. It will reflect by itself around us and will light the hearts of others.

What we have to do: not hate anyone.
– Baba Hari Dass

To Be Present Is To Be Free

May we free our minds through being present – unoccupied – in the moment. Our thoughts and beliefs can be like mud in water. They often distort or block our ability to see beauty - possibility - actuality - and divinity. When the water is clear, the sun illuminates the waves and fishes floating about. When the water is muddy, you see only the mud.

Our heart is like clear blue-green water. When we open ourselves to the moment, then our hearts reflect love and beauty outward into the world.

To the illumined man or woman,
A clod of dirt, a stone, and gold are the same.
– *Bhagavad Gita*

    *   *   *

She's playing in my heart.
Whatever I think, I think Her name.
– Ramprasad

All Life Is God

May we notice the Sacredness of all life today.

Take a bite of food; it becomes your bones and blood. Breathe in; the air energizes your cells and gives you strength to move. Drink water; you are over 80% water. Notice the flame burning in your candles; this light of fire is the same energy that transforms and feeds all life. Look at the friend by your side; this being warms your heart when you are blue. All living life feeds us - air, earth, water, fire, friendship. All of it is God.

Love is the reward of love. May you notice love in the gifts all around you. May you embody love, and be love, for truly love is the greatest healing energy in life, and love is the reward of love. All life is God.

All fear is a fabrication. So when fear talks to you, just remember that it's a fabrication and be disinterested in it. It's not even a story you like to hear, so why would you listen to it?
– Maticintin

*   *   *

Work is love made visible.
– *Daily Guru*

Fear is love for oneself

Fear arises to try to protect you when the mind perceives that you need help. Fear is natural and is a very powerful source of energy that arises within us. However, if we do not harness it with awareness and choice, then it can exhaust us and paralyze our lives.

When fear arises, may we breathe in deeply, breathe out all your air and then breathe our more, and then again breathe in very deeply. We can choose to use the energy of fear to fill our lives with that which we love.

Fear is powerful life-energy that we can use to create all that we dream of. It arises usually when we feel threatened in some way, but often this fear is based on a past situation that is no longer present or based on a limiting or false inner belief (i.e., "He will hate me if he sees the real me").

As you learn to trust God, then fear loses such a tight grip on you, because your sites are on something very big.

Breathe in love, and fill up your heart and chest. Breathe out fear. Do this for a few minutes. Then stand up, walk outside, and choose courage. In that very moment, begin to act according to love. Use your life's energy to create and sustain your dreams. Everytime you walk through the fear, you make that habit a little less strong, and it starts to change your life.

May you live love.

Every day, whether we see it or not, we have a choice of two alternatives in what we do, say, and think. These alternatives are: what is pleasant and what is beneficial.
– Eknath Easwaran

* * *

I can change. I can live out my imagination instead of my memory. I can tie myself to my limitless potential instead of my limiting past.
– Stephen Covey

* * *

No worry, no hurry, no sorry.
– a monk in Hawaii, with a peaceful look in his eye

Pleasant and Beneficial

May we see the good points and build life around those.

May we see with imagination rather than memory.

May we believe in dreams and possibilities rather than limits or doubts.

Will you worship that which is negative or limiting - or will you worship that which is pleasant and beneficial? That which is in your thoughts all day long is that which you worship. Notice your thoughts. For 30 days, observe your thoughts. Are they mostly negative and whiny? Or are they celebratory? Or grateful?

May we worship God over our own mind (fear/analysis), and may we fill our life with that which is healing, wholesome, and holy.

Breathe in peace. Breathe out and know that you deserve all that you would give to those whom you love and all that you would give to God.

Wherever you go, you will always
bear yourself about you,
and so you will always find yourself.
– Thomas A Kempis

*   *   *

I think it's a mistake to ever look for hope outside of one's self. One day the house smells of fresh bread, the next of smoke and blood. One day you faint because the gardener cuts his finger off, within a week you're climbing over corpses of children bombed in a subway. What hope can there be if that is so?...I think one must finally take one's life in one's arms.
– Arthur Miller, from *"After the Fall"*

Look Within

May we realize that negativity outside of us is a projection of something within us that may require forgiveness or care and love. Wounds from times when people have been mean to us need our own tender care and love to heal now. This love comes truly from God, but we can consciously ask that it come into our own heart and life.

Rather than seek outside ourselves for anything, or blame anything outside ourselves for our pain, may we realize that pain comes from our thoughts and wounded hearts. A lot of people use pain as a power play to get revenge on someone else, or at least to get people's attention and time. Sometimes we do truly need to ask for help, but just notice when people are actually using pain to achieve something such as revenge. This lesson is simple but not easy. We project nearly everything outside of ourselves until we learn not to, and we project our needs outside of ourselves as well (i.e., onto food, or drugs, or relationships, or sex, etc) until we realize that God is our true source and sustenance.

May we give ourselves the forgiveness that will begin to heal the pains of our wounds and our beliefs in separation.

May God take your pain and fill your heart with joy, peace, and loving-kindness. Your God is within your own heart: look within and be free.

One who would be serene and pure
needs but one thing, nonattachment.
– Meister Eckhart

*   *   *

"Internalize everything, externalize nothing...The expression of hate, negativity, or any negative thought, feeling, or state results when you reach a level of resistance and do not work through it. Expression of negative feelings builds or reinforces blocks; work overcomes them....How you use food is more important than what you eat."
– Rudi, *Spiritual Cannibalism*, p.44

Non-attachment

Let go of everything. We can practice this.

From a space of pure being, of acceptance, may we experience a deep abiding peace.

This is the peace of divinity that sits like an ocean deep within your own heart. It is the core of every being's heart, and it is your source and truest sustenance. It permeates all life and beyond. When you sit in awareness of this deep ocean of love within your heart, then the waves on the surface do not shake you up as they otherwise would. You can observe the waves, and roll with the waves, but your being is very deep and still and strong - a sacred ocean of love.

May you always gaze both inward to your Beloved deep in your spiritual heart as well as outward to your Beloved in the world of forms.

You have a beautiful heart.
— Swami Chetanananda

*   *   *

You are the Sun in drag.
You are God hiding from yourself.
— Hafiz

*   *   *

There are many paths to enlightenment.
Be sure to take the one with a heart.
— Lao Tzu

You Are God Hiding From Yourself

May you know that you have a beautiful heart, that you are so valuable and sacred.

When you know this, then your heart can begin to feel a deep peace and joy. You can relax in a way that you have not ever yet known. This does not mean inaction; it simply means compassionate action with deep relaxation, remaining centered deep in your heart, where God resides.

View all life with your eyes always on your Sacred Heart. When this is your view, you do not need to commit crimes or harm life in the same ways, for you do not need to act or react out of need or a sense of lack. Instead, you desire to honor the value of life.

We have all made mistakes, and we have all experienced misfortune. We are all everything.

You are God hiding from yourself. Know it, live it.

You don't need to hide or pretend to be less or more than others, anymore.

To the eye of the seer every leaf of the tree is a page of the Holy book that contains divine revelation, and he is inspired every moment of his life by constantly reading and understanding the holy script of nature.
– from *The Sufi Message of Hazrat Inayat Khan, Vol. 1, Sufi Thoughts*

*   *   *

What I know in my bones is that I forgot to take time to remember what I know. The world is holy. We are holy. All life is holy. Daily prayers are delivered on the lips of breaking waves, the whisperings of grasses, the shimmering of leaves.
– Terry Tempest Williams

*   *   *

The greatness of a nation and its moral progress can be determined by the way it treats its animals.
– Mohandas Gandhi

Nature

When you behold nature, may you see God, for all of it is God's creation – born of God's heart and essence. All of it is a gift that by its divine essence deserves cherishing and stewardship.

Once a man who labels himself as a devoted Christian said, "To hell with them [animals]...That's what they're there for [for humans to consume]." He did not recognize that animals might have a right to their own lives and to a natural, organic quality of life.

Please remember how Native peoples honor animals. Even though they may eat animals, they pray over them, feel deep gratitude for them, allow them to live freely and humanely, kill them humanely, and even view the animals as their own relatives.

The plants and animals are made of the same life essence as we are. They are our relatives, and because of the nature of the modern world, we have a responsibility to be their stewards, not their abusers.

May we see God in all nature, for truly God created it all and feeds us beauty and healing life energy everywhere we turn. Not only humans are divine; all life is divine.

Be a lamp unto yourself.
– Buddha

*   *   *

Of the good in you I can speak, but not of the evil. For what is evil but good tortured by its own hunger and thirst?...You are good when you strive to give of yourself. Yet you are not evil when you seek gain for yourself. For when you strive for gain you are but a root that clings to the earth and sucks at her breast...You are good in countless ways, and you are not evil when you are not good...But let NOT him who longs much say to him who longs little," Wherefore are you slow and halting?"
 For the truly good ask NOT the naked, "Where is your garment?" nor the houseless, "What has befallen your house?"
– Kahlil Gibran, *The Prophet*, 78

Do not compare, for all life is divine

Friends, may we not compare our own path with that of others, for each path is carried by the same longing and carries us toward the same destination, in its own unique and beauty-filled way, in its own time, trusting God as we are able to.

When we are ready, may we say, "My heart is ready, O God, my heart is ready" but let us not force that on others who are not ready or who have a different path, but only share and enjoy each moment, with care, trust, and surrender.

Live your life, follow your heart, and serve as an example and a light for all the world. When others are ready, according to God's grace, they will evolve and grow.

Devotion brings an end to the war within your being.
 – Beloved Ma Jaya Sati Bhagavati

*   *   *

Beliefs separate. Loving thoughts unite.
 – Paul Ferrini

Worship Love

May we worship love more than the comparing mind. Some moments this could really be challenging. However, let us simply try our best. Every time we notice judgment or comparisons or negative beliefs, may we instead simply love, to the best of our ability. One way that we can do this is to start a gratitude list. Everyday, list 10 different things you are grateful for. In difficult moments, list as many things as possible in that moment that you are grateful for.

All life is simultaneously unique and one. Judgment is a habit, made of fear. It is a belief that we are not good enough as we are. Judgment arises when we do not see the depths of our own beauty. Ma Jaya Sati Bhagavati teaches us that "jealousy is the lack of ability to see your own beauty." Jealousy is the companion of judgment; they walk hand in hand.

"...one caterpillar, a thousand hairs of God. So know constantly that this is only you, God, empty and awake and eternally free as the unnumerable atoms of emptiness everywhere."
– Jack Kerouac

*   *   *

"Finally the autumn rains, all-night gales of soaking rain as I lie warm as toast in my sleeping bag and the mornings open cold wild fall days with high wind, racing fogs, racing clouds, sudden bright sun, pristine light on hill patches and my fire crackling as I exult and sing at the top of my voice. What strange sweet thoughts come to you in the mountain solitudes! One night I realized that when you give people understanding and encouragement a funny meek little childish look abashes their eyes...lambies all over the world. For when you realize that God is Everything, you know that you've got to love everything no matter how bad it is, in the ultimate sense it was neither good or bad, it was just WHAT WAS, that is, what was made to appear... ...silence itself is the sound of diamonds which can cut through anything, the sound of Holy Emptiness, the sound of extinction and bliss, that graveyard silence which is like the silence of an infant's smile, the sound of eternity, of the blessedness surely to be believed, the sound of nothing-ever-happened-except-God...'Ts only the Golden Eternity of God's Mind so practice kindness and sympathy, remember that men are not responsible themselves as men for their ignorance and unkindness, they should be pitied, God does pity it, because who says anything about anything since everything is just what it is, free of interpretations..."
– Jack Kerouac, *Lonesome Traveler*, p.133

Darkness Closes The Heart

Friends, may we realize that when life becomes heavy and sticky, that we can look back and see whether this is a false belief that we have accepted as true (e.g., "I am unlovable" or "Life is terribly hard"), or judgments of the way things "should" be (e.g., "I can only be happy if..."), or something in our life that we need to change (e.g., "I know I am a good person so do not deserve to live with mean people"). Negativity is an indicator that something needs to change, and this change nearly always begins within. It is sometimes known as "divine discontent." This means that it is our divine guidance toward bringing more light and joy into our life.

When life feels heavy, may we discover that which needs to shift – whether a belief, circumstance, attitude, or other thing – and then may we do something that will restore joy to our being: meditation/prayer, or walking through the woods, or doing something kind for another person, or taking a bubble bath, or watching a funny movie, or just smiling at someone - anything that our heart knows will bring us lightness and joy.

Dark beliefs crowd out the love in one's heart, because the heart becomes thick, cloudy, and heavy with pain. Find a safe space, alone or with someone you can trust. Then, focus on something that shall restore your openness of heart, to let that innate Love again flow through you. Give tenderness toward oneself or whoever is in a space of pain or darkness. Pray. Most often, a hug, a walk, a bubble bath, or a smile will help someone better than advice (unless asked for). Simply hold the space for them to experience whatever they need to experience without trying to fix, heal, or alter it. We do not need to play God; that is for God to do. With our love, let us be an equal and a friend. Let us hold someone's hand, offer a shoulder, and be there for him or her, in pleasant as well as difficult times.

Identify with Love and you are safe.
Identify with Love and you are home.
Identify with Love and find your Self.
– *A Course In Miracles*

       *   *   *

A tree is known by its fruit; we by our deeds.
A good deed is never lost; one who sows courtesy
reaps friendship, and one who plants kindness gathers love.
– Saint Basil

I Am Love

Love will bring love, and fear will bring fear. That which we pay attention to grows stronger in our lives. That which we pay attention to is that which we worship.

When we go within our hearts, in prayer or meditation, we can listen for the peaceful voice within. Inside our hearts there is so much space that can come up to the surface and bring us bliss.

When you feel afraid, wrap yourself up in the love that you need. May you find it within your own heart: you deserve love and all that you dream of.

Giving love to others or yourself will bring you love, and giving negativity to others or yourself will bring more negativity to your life. May we choose with awareness in each moment.

We do not believe in ourselves until someone reveals that deep inside us something is valuable, worth listening to, worthy of our trust, sacred to our touch. Once we believe in ourselves we can risk curiosity, wonder, spontaneous delight or any experience that reveals the human spirit
– EE Cummings

*   *   *

Be as loving as you can towards all of life and all of its expressions and that way you lift the level of the sea, the ocean, and by the lifting of the sea, you lift all of the ships at sea.
– David R Hawkins

Kindness Will Lift A Heart

May we allow ourselves to feel the pain that may arise when someone is unkind to us, but let us know that we do not have to respond that same way. In other words, people act unkind either when they lack awareness, when they are in pain themselves, or when they want to hurt you. But it is always our choice and our ability whether or not we shall accept what they offer us. We do not have to accept chaos, hell, or pain from another human being. We can care for ourselves as best possible.

Also, this will give us the space and peace we need in order to be able to have compassion for their own suffering, for it is only a being who suffers (or who is ignorant, which is nearly all of us unfortunately) who harms another being. Within our own lives, we can always choose something better: to be kind, to the best of our ability. This does not stay mean to stay in a house with an abuser. It means to leave that house but to not be tormented by what "someone tried to do to me" because we realize that that person has some serious problems to face. You, yourself, can be free of that. It is your choice. Also, you do not have to save mean or tormented people. That is in God's hands. Be kind to yourself, as your greatest responsibility is to yourself. From there, be kind to others (on the condition that you are not harmed in the process).

Kindness will always lift a heart, and one thing that is much needed in this world today, is lifted hearts.

May we lift hearts through kindness and care, and may we be the friends and stewards of all life – all equal, all one family, all one.

The wonderful thing about spiritual work is that within our practice there are no issues and agendas. You're not here trying to correct anything about yourself, and I'm definitely not here trying to correct you. Spiritual practice is about being able to feel the essence of yourself, your own creative energy, and to awaken and continuously extend that energy to its limits, if you can ever find any.
– Swami Chetanananda, Santa Monica, Jan 22, 2000

*   *   *

"...continuously dwell with your attention in the field of now, the field itself. Let the world happen. Let it happen...it's great. Let the forms come and go as they will. No form stays for that long...You enjoy the play of form around you, then the fear of loss is no longer there. Why is there the fear of loss? Because there is the identification with some content, and there's the fear that if I lose that, I lose part of who I am. That's the fear of loss...You can see what a miraculous transformation it is when humans no longer live dominated by fear. My God! You can actually live in a state of joy and aliveness continuously no matter what arises, because what arises isn't that important. It's a form. It's short-lived. It's a play of phenomenal existence. It's the universe playing with form...Let it play with form. You yourself become a participant in the play of form. You can create without self-seeking. Then you create beautifully. But when you create and there is self-seeking in it, there's a negative energy field in it. I need, I want, I must have, without that I am nobody, oh I mustn't lose that...
– Eckhart Tolle

Live Life In This Moment, With Passion

Friends, when we experience loss we feel deep passion, deep emotion. In day-to-day life, we are encouraged to stifle our passion, and it is only in loss that we are socially allowed to express it - temporarily.

We must allow our passion to arise, express it in compassionate action, let it out! Allow yourself to feel the passion that you feel everyday, not just when you lose or are about to lose that which you love. This is the way of "beginner mind" – open to possibility, present, aware, expressive, intuitive. All the parts of your being open and move when you live holistically. Holistic = whole = holy.

Express your deep passion as compassionate action. This is all about energy - how you direct it, what you do with it...As Swami Rudrananda taught, "Does life consume you, or do you consume life?" Passion is very strong, so with conscious choice we can guide our life energy toward incredible acts of beauty, creation, care, and so forth.

May you ride the waves of each moment, with all your passion, expressed as compassionate action.

*   *   *
God blesses you every moment;
may you experience the depths of this within your own life.

About The Author

Heather Havey is co-founder of Friends For Compassionate Earth Awareness and Paradise Earth Gardens, located in Sebastian, Florida. She is a naturalist and a veganic (vegan organic) farmer who lives by a philosophy of care and non-harm toward all life forms, to the best of one's awareness and ability.

Heather holds a M.A. in Transpersonal Psychology, and she is a licensed yoga teacher in Hatha, Kundalini, and Kali Natha lineages of yoga. She teaches yoga, meditation, partner yoga, nonviolent communication, conflict resolution, veganic farming and sustainability, and living foods lifestyle classes. She has taught yoga and meditation in prisons, homeless shelters, and hospices for many years. Jesus, Neem Karoli Baba, Ma Jaya Sati Bhagavati, Jaya Devi Bhagavati, Mother Teresa, Buddha, Gandhi, Coretta Scott King, and Martin Luther King, Jr. are her most important influences and spiritual teachers, to whom she is infinitely grateful.

For fun, she likes to swim in the ocean, grow plants, and write poetry. Also, she surfs, backpacks, kayaks, snorkels, sails, serves others, helps to teach families how to grow food, and appreciates all of the myriad and sacred forms of life.

Visit her: **www.peacethroughkindness.com**

"Sana nagai bikeh hozho."
"May you walk in beauty, always."
(Navajo philosophy)

www.ingramcontent.com/pod-product-compliance
Lightning Source LLC
Chambersburg PA
CBHW021024090426
42738CB00007B/894